The Accounts

Thirty Years of
PHOENIX POETS

KATIE PETERSON

The Accounts

THE UNIVERSITY OF CHICAGO PRESS

Chicago & London

KATIE PETERSON is professor of the practice of poetry at Tufts University. She is the author of two other collections of poetry, *This One Tree* and *Permission*. She was born in California.

The University of Chicago Press, Chicago 60637
The University of Chicago Press, Ltd., London
© 2013 by The University of Chicago
All rights reserved. Published 2013.
Printed in the United States of America

22 21 20 19 18 17 16 15 14 13   1 2 3 4 5

ISBN-13: 978-0-226-06266-2 (paper)
ISBN-13: 978-0-226-06283-9 (e-book)

Library of Congress Cataloging-in-Publication Data
Peterson, Katie, 1974– author.
    [Poems. Selections]
    The accounts / Katie Peterson.
        pages cm. — (Phoenix poets series)
    Poems.
    ISBN: 978-0-226-06266-2 (paperback : alkaline paper) —
    ISBN: 978-0-226-06283-9 (e-book)
    I. Title. II. Series: Phoenix poets.
    PS3616.E8429A63 2013
    811'.6 — dc23

                                    2012048350

♾ This paper meets the requirements of ANSI/NISO Z39.48-1992 (Permanence of Paper).

For My Father

I cannot tell how Eternity seems. It sweeps around me like a sea.

Emily Dickinson

CONTENTS

THREE: I AM THE MIDDLE

ACKNOWLEDGMENTS

Grateful acknowledgment is given to the editors of the following publications in which some of the poems in this book previously appeared, or will appear, sometimes in different versions:

Boston Review: "Argument about the Beginning"
www.bostonreview.net: "Sore Throat"
Guernica, A Magazine of Art & Politics (www.guernicamag.com): "Enough"
Harvard Advocate: "Wilderness," "Snake"
Kenyon Review: "Elegy," "Rest"
Memorious, A Journal of New Verse and Fiction (www.memorious. org): "The Accounts"

"The Accounts," the winner of the 2011 Memorious Art Song Contest, was set to music for soprano and ensemble by Luke Gullickson, and performed for the first time on September 24, 2011, in Chicago, Illinois, as part of *Singers on New Ground: Ars Poetica II.*

The author wishes to thank Deep Springs College, the Foundation for Contemporary Arts, the Radcliffe Institute for Advanced Study, and Yaddo for making this work possible. The author also wishes to thank Louise Glück and Sandra Lim for invaluable help with the completion of the manuscript.

One

Spring

SPRING

I have been trying to read *King Lear*. End up drinking
red wine, and talking about the tropics.
Thought there might be a poem in the play,
maybe the way he talks about the button
on his coat before he dies standing, carrying
the body of the hanged. Maybe the part
where she refuses to bargain and the maps
on the table are redrawn.

———

I am sleeping. Elsewhere, you are finishing *Tess
of the d'Urbervilles*, those last chapters, before they end
up at Stonehenge, and Angel says to Tess
*Sleepy my dear I think you are lying
on the altar.* The part where the book lets them
hold each other, without sleepwalking
or lies. Angel has traded in his harp
for a tin kettle and bread. They picnic in a damask-curtained bed,
a fugitive and an accomplice. I may be turning
toward the branch of apple blossom bearing its burden
of the raindrops in an even more buoyant aspect
than the night before. Now you are the caretaker,
finding Tess's fine silk stockings draped
on the damask coverlet in the house they squat in,
giving both of them away.

———

The tree in the side yard not
yet in the kind of flower to release it
and uncover it again. Everything, everything, and before
everything the possibility of something else,
the moment when a moral gets minced by an account
a body makes of any other body,
and time takes place instead of taking time.
Cordelia with the armies of her husband
scouring the unharvested corn of her homeland
for her naked, wandering, delusional father.
Tess at the dairy, good at her job. Angel
in the field, his fingers on the strings of his harp.
You carrying me into a lake in August,
the summer my mother left the earth.

ELEGY

At the border between winter
and spring, at the house I am living in,
outside the window
in the bedroom, closest to the bed,
a branch I thought of as near dead
comes into a cascade of flowers
the color of champagne.

For weeks, I couldn't think of the right
figure from myth.
I rejected the seeds of the pomegranate.
I rejected the mirror, rejected
going in drag toward the laurel
and calling it mine.
I wanted a woman who grabs.

I bought a camera, and began to save
the sound of the wind through fences,
to layer it over water
running the course of an icy creek
in the desert, but I couldn't keep
the scent of sage rising with the rain
across a rock covered with lichen.

All winter that dark arm
scratched my window, paying no

attention to my appetite for sleep.
I could have ripped it right out.
Something kept me from that.
Judgment is preferable to faithfulness.
A pair of handcuffs better than a ring.

The mistake other people make,
I won't: because the rules have changed,
there is nothing beautiful to obey.
For three hundred years an island lost
the ability to make pottery on a wheel.
They looted ruins that had been houses once.
But they knew they had been houses.

I refused the pomegranate, I took
back the mirror, but I took from
the pomegranate its difficulty, its bitter
extraction. From the mirror, I took
its appetite for change.
The laurel had been my address.
I changed it.

I can't say that I'll stay up all night
waiting for the ghost, but I will promise
a thing more difficult:
If she asks, I will do what she says.
So when I fail her, you will know
exactly how to punish me.

ARGUMENT ABOUT HEAVEN

As a child, I was taken
to look at a mountain, every year,
in the summer.

I was only willing to say:
nothing terrifying happens to the good

The lookout road opened
when the snowpack melted, late
in the season

Others have argued for green fields

Every year my father pointed to the mountain.

I couldn't see that far—meaning, I suppose,
I didn't want to—

His finger traced a rivulet toward a source
high in a crease where two mountains met.
His thumbprint on
the site where he had camped.

When others speak of green fields,
I get sick.

A map etched in metal with the names
of all the mountains in the range
and a line of ridge representing the crest—
we leaned against that.

Fantasies I've tried recently to kill: happy
family, heaven

I liked to trace that ridge with my ring
finger, on my left hand, the one
I wrote with, and then do the same
in the air, across the original. Later, in the car,
with my eyes shut, I tried again, on the window,
as we drove across the bay.

Shouldn't goodness be rewarded
with the absence of terror?

We went to fish, not to climb.
At Deadman Creek, my father
baited his hook while half a dozen
sucked the blood from his hand.

But I have seen the shape green fields
make in the eye,
like a casino in a small town.

One year we didn't have time
to go to the mountain.

That morning, we had fished a lake for nothing.
The night before, we played poker, but the children
wanted to make everything wild.

Too many wild cards kill the competition.

The adults becoming frustrated
with the children playing their games,
though it would be wrong to say
we had no regard for rules.

I begged to see the mountain.

But it is punishment that governs the field.

That meant I asked once, on behalf of someone else,
but experienced my own disappointment.

You're not a farmer—the field
doesn't pay for you. You pay for the field.

The mountain isn't a bottomless well.
You know you have to pay your tribute.

The good breathe so deeply, it is like eating—

your tribute is your presence, the coinage
of your person—

those from whom the burden has been lifted—

though the country you drive through is beautiful
with a range of blues the envy of the Netherlands—

their hands rest at their sides—

it is not the mountain—

and you can live like that.

SORE THROAT

Sick in bed with a sore throat,
I can't get out of my mind
the image of the cat
harpsichord from the eighteenth century,
soothing a prince with laughter.

It worked like this: the tails of them attached
to the strings of the instrument
were pulled by different notes, and the difference
between the way the cats
cried was music.

A shadow is only a shape.
Which is why certain individuals
can put their hands in light
and make them birds, can say in shadow
what they can't in light.

The tiny branches of the hedge
in the yard that separates
my house from the next
look like the rib bones of a bird
when the sun hits lunch.

The world, they say, is best for a nest
but no good for a flying place.
Come back, I say to my dead,
and the branches don't even graze
the window, when I eat it hurts.

ARGUMENT ABOUT APPETITE

When you say, *imagine yourself
in a safe green place*, I lie
on her grave, looking up
at the inscription in the monument
where my father's date will go.

The question of alignment
complicates the spiritual writings
of the ancients.

Fog drifts in. We are safer, I think,
without sunlight, without

St. John of the Cross
keeping his head up straight,
so his soul, which he calls
the body of the bride
would be looking up,
not just the eyes.

Eleven o'clock in the morning
and the whole day ahead.

Or that each pose in the series
proceeds to headstand
or standing. In the arm balance

I am inside an anxious quiet

called Crow, the knees nest
in the upper arms, and the head
stays low

I think I have always been there.

You should breathe into the hands.
You should remove the bones
of the hands and replace them
with adamantine chains.

Definition of picnic: excursion to the country
taking food to be eaten outside

The earth takes the soul out of alignment.
The body takes the soul
fishing for nothing in a shitty river

Originally, a meal to which everyone
brought their own share

In one pose, the hands
reach back to catch the toes.
You have become a bow.

Later, any assemblage, an anthology,
in the nineteenth century, one guide
to the wild flowers of a private park
in England called Best Man's End
was called End's Picnic. You should see

There are many practices,

the specimens, dried and pressed,
identified not only by name
but by the approximate
time of their plucking.

The trick is practicing every day
what it is you practice,

an assiduous acquisition, a rape

to continue on the path.
Often, in the imagination of these texts,

determined by the perfection of the petals,
a lack of tatter,
and the sturdiness of the stem

the spiritual workday is night

To the picnic I bring my body,

the eyes have a meaning past use,

and little else, I am so thirsty,

the question is are you saved

I open my mouth to the fog

because you pay attention?

THE REPLACEMENT

It is difficult to believe, but before
the Japanese maple oriented
the corner of the brick front
porch, before the roots
drank up the minerals
of rich dirt, and the branches
spread into hands and smaller
hands, under the porchlight,
which still drops
a circle of its orange light
evenly across uneven
leaves, as the tree met the earth
unwillingly, transplanted from a garden
where all it had to do
was be like anything near it that resembled it,
since that is how so many lives
begin, especially the decorative,
which are not less because they are not deep,
as, literally, these roots are not deep enough,
my mother planted a rosebush
which thrived so before it died
we walked on petals three seasons of the year.
And though this was California,
such behavior of a plant could still
be understood as the excess
of what a person tending

the garden should expect.
To hold on to one thing to
the excess of all else
resembles being
attached to nothing at all.
The years passed;
the replacement grew refulgent.

EARTH

I didn't come here to make speeches.
I didn't come here to make trouble.
I didn't come here to be
somebody's mother.
I didn't come here to make friends.
I didn't come here to teach.
I didn't come here to drag the space heater
from the house in summer with an extension
cord out to the orchard because
the peach trees we planted
in a climate that couldn't take them
didn't thrive, couldn't sweeten
their fruit in a place like this.

WHEN FRUIT AND FLOWERS
HUNG THICK FALLING

Never a gardener, she
became interested

in gardening. The dying
are known to

make estranging
decisions

about the disclosure
of information.

Everyone knew
where the report

cards were, but the marriage
license proved difficult

to locate. Tomato
and potato vines crawled

up different stakes
in the same barrel,

and she tended
equally the decorative

plants, the lobelia and alyssum
fringing and clinging to

the edges, in the sun
under a visor

fuzzy with the terry
cloth of enough

vacations to forget
the number, to wear

the lettering
into half-glyphs insinuating

but not stating
the location of past

happiness. She knelt,
hinged

at the waist,
thrust

her hands in dirt
feeling for roots

even when
they no longer

needed
tending, even

when fruit and flowers
hung thick falling.

ALLIED ARTS

You walked around the corner to get to the artists,
their shops organized around a courtyard
and in the middle stood a fountain
in the midst of hedges organized
in the shape of a star,
and when you looked down you were surrounded
by tiles painted with sea horses
and single vines that ended
in a flower that was half-daisy, daisy
with a smaller, darker center, with longer
petals, and at the base of the flower,
the stalk just ended, as if it were cut.
You were left to imagine the root, if you chose,
which, if it had existed, could have stretched
into another tile, as the tile of the sea horse
would have stretched into the sea horse mother.
At the end of the furthest corridor,
with the curve of a Spanish arch, past the walk
which had roses on either side
named for adults you could ask questions about,
for example, Mary Todd Lincoln,
who in the movie moment you remember
said she had a headache
when a period was what she meant, at the end
of that walk the woodworker
crafts your family a claw-footed table,

matching it to chairs
with high backs, and a carving like a mustache,
a smooth stroke of blankness
against a background of leaves and vines.
You are watching the dust rise from the tool
he's using to make the surface flat.
You don't have a name
for that, you are not
holding anyone's hand, and the sound
of what will stand
at the center of the room
where you will eat
for years gets finished.

ARGUMENT ABOUT THE BEGINNING

The birth of a daughter

The loneliness, the absence, the vacancy, the illness

is different from the birth of a son. Ask the womb

where the tree was

Ask the forceps, the anesthetic

becomes a circle of light

Ask the army

and it's not so bad, it's not like a field

of husbands in the waiting room

after the crops are cut:

Degrees of happiness are a ludicrous way

new growth: a garden

of understanding happiness

of lettuces or a garden for the eye

but it is the only way, I think,

planted with perennials

Remember how the world was made?

Even to leave the circle bare,
a form of worshipping the sun
to give the sun that circle
completely, to deed
that circle to the sun

By dividing.

A place is not what it is

Sky from the waters

A place is what it makes possible,

It is not revealed in the account

The grass dies but the sun thrives, for example

but I bet God loved the waters

for example, a clearing in a forest for a house

more than he loved

the tide pulling out

what he separated them from.

ENOUGH

So many forget-me-nots, with their white centers,
scattered, you'd say, if there weren't
so many everywhere, as many as the stars
last night in between the branches
above the porch, behind the house.
Was it an argument or were there just
things they had to say?
I could have faith in so many creatures—
the old setter from the neighbor yard
who follows me around the corner
and no longer, the chick with its new beak
just past breakable whose lighter top feathers
have a bit of flight, any mother bear—
you say things and the next day
it's like they don't matter, we want our faces
to alter though we don't want to get older, neither
do we want to get younger, repetition
with less knowledge is ridiculous,
just ask the Greeks, you get to keep
being a tree but without the branch
that showed the sky your starlike shape?
I don't think so. Steadiness can be useful,
but my loyalty loves a form
that will follow me through changes.
At a diagonal the dark woods
on the back slope have enough space

to walk between, not enough to hide.
He looks into them
and writes notes to his mother, she
looks into them and finds alignment,
or looks for what she wants.
She has a human skeleton on her desk.
He has a protractor. I had wishes
for both of them yesterday
but the weather has become so kindly,
so temperate, I forget what blessings
they don't think they have.

BEAUTY

I was teaching you about beauty.
You and some other people. I used
a Buddha, and the one
I produced came from a long distance,
green metal, sedate, no facial

expression. With pursed lips. In the light
of the desert, the crevasses
of its cheeks, its merry
headdress, looked like wrinkles,
if a child who made up rules

to all the games he chose to play
could show a kind of age. My example
of the opposite was DNA.
The desire to protect what I believed
was beautiful—a fact

I placed before all of us
on the table. I placed it next to this statement:
what is beautiful excludes.
A hand gesture with my left, careless, a near obscenity.
You laughed. Sun finding the dust on half

a dozen scientific instruments: an early
seismograph, a rusty barometer,

and the photos of the first
dwellers, next to lists of donors
who allow our operations

to continue. Your fellow students
asleep. Maybe a few
in dreams of labor, in dreams of pulling
a calf just born in the reeds
from the mouth of a coyote.

You I exclude. You asked
about those who destroy
what they find beautiful.
I will tell this story
until I have your answer.

REST

When I look at the field it is still
the field of possibility—
frost comes, and the heat lifts
to see it melt, to see the heat
of the sun persist
even though winter is on the way.
I am more optimistic those days
when the weather
is unseasonable, Indian summer, this
to me is the dregs
of a thing, it is a wedding ring
in the mind after
a sexual dream. The point
of sex is for both
parties to perform the same
activity, according to the poet
who is afraid of death
the way he is afraid of the sun.
But he sees himself
and his object running
through a gate, not a field.

WILDERNESS

In the cities where the waste would exist in the future, no vista
but signage. Long past the time it took a law to change
the institutions would tell visitors *translate the instructions*
in case they couldn't understand *into your own tongue.*
My car went off the road once where it curves
because an antelope looked like the dusk
and I was driving into the dusk to catch a plane. I mean I didn't
want to stop. The blue shadow in the middle
distance a band of ice that cut the middle out of eyesight,
out of those mountains, out of everything: no middle here.
Back at the ranch, behind the house, you and I
sat around the spool watching the moon's
deckle edge unchange for one entire warm spring night.
You left your jacket, didn't come to get it for a day.
One cleared field adjacent to a field that grew wild.
More ravens in the vicinity of it than persons.
The road is the beginning of the valley but the pass
it passes through is so tiring the eye
concentrates on its own failure and can't imagine the rest.

Two   The Body

THE GARDEN

It was like this: she wanted the garden
but she didn't want the garden.
A narrative of progress: when she did well,
she got a bed by the wall, not the window,
by the door where visitors came,
not the window that looked on to the garden.

The person who was dying more
deserved the garden, though at times she suspected
some algorithm between the dying
and the difficult, that the people in charge
had a system, that the reward of the garden
wasn't always earned. But by July,

that summer, when the chemo
became so much a part of her system
on the scans they couldn't tell
the difference between blood and poison, they
both lit up: she lucked
into the garden because the nurse

who dressed in drag thought she carried
herself like Gloria Swanson, thriving
in a state of languishing. Never any question
she deserved the garden, as she said, though you can't
smell them through the glass, the lilacs
are the only things to look at in this place. She meant the earth.

NEST

The week my mother died, my father
worked all afternoon under the patio
umbrella just outside the family
room where we had put her temporary
bed, for the sun, and the sound
of the blue jays keeping the robins
from the feeder, filled with seeds
and shaped like a schoolhouse.

Above his head, a robin's nest
in an upper corner, because,
as my brother said, they trusted him,
he billed his hours there,
when you watched his hand
from a little distance, from a car
coming into the driveway, after an errand,
amazing that the table didn't jitter.

We never saw the mother, she must
have come and gone at night, or so
quickly, or when none of us
was looking. My father said he hadn't
seen her, either. He is no predator.
When he shakes the table it is a mistake
not an accident. He did what he always
did: acted like he wasn't even there,
and somehow kept everyone away.

FORESIGHT

The robin who built this nest
gambled with the umbrella. The table
tends to rattle, especially when more
than two talk at it. But it's understandable:
the likelier location, the tree

in front of me, an Eastern redbud, roots
to the left, blooms too heavily on the right, splays
from the trunk like an octopus
not a starfish, with an activity
not exactly about staying put, not exactly
about getting where it should: straight up. Not even hummingbirds

with their wings using all the intervals
of minutes, every slice smaller,
being cut through with another slice,
temporary homes in hunger itself, don't source
their intoxication from these sweet
unbalanced buds, half flower, half unfinished
leaf, not even hummingbirds believe in the tree,

or have confidence, as I know the green
belly of the smallest sweet seeking
bird doesn't get
his nectar from that tree,
all birds of that kind, and, indeed,
all birds with a mind seek elsewhere what they seek.

The placement of this nest,
a gamble. But building the nest wasn't a gamble.
The making of the nest started in the mind
of the mother before a place in the world
was found. That wasn't wrong. There weren't guarantees.
What we call instinct, she called foresight,

with no place to put it; what we call
composition, she calls design.
What we call priorities, she calls instinct
or doesn't call anything at all.

SYMBOL

Picture of the nest, taken by the right hand
of my sister, in the rafters
of the umbrella next to the house where we were raised.
When my father saw the picture,
he said it was a symbol.

Weird how social the week of death.
We carried our chitchat around like candy.
For days I carried the color
of the lilacs in the garden of the cancer
ward, purple as glamour.

Which was not a symbol. Any more
than the dressing table
of Marilyn Monroe with its eye creams
and foundation made a picture
of useless labor.
She had to get up in the morning.

When he said it was a symbol, he meant life,
a turnaround. I hoped
he meant something else, a syllable,
part of the whole, something to emphasize
on the lips. Or sign, as yet unreadable, but multiple in meaning,
readable by other better maybe even winged
ordained or paid authority figures.

Why did I hope anything for him?
As if his understanding had been
my possession, or worse, a product
of my teaching, an answer
to some predestined question.
He just wanted to have something to say.

A POTTER

You thought of a potter, though the hollow
wasn't made by any hand. Wasn't spun,
though looked it. Wasn't clay
but what clay has at times been mixed into
to make a house. Of a wheel,
of the sound of a hollow made at a speed
governed by a hand, like the hollow spring
makes in the winter heart,
the heart that's learned to be generous
in scarcity, only to emerge
into a country where money is no object.
You thought of a potter because the making
of the nest fell all over the nest
as an understanding, the gathering
from materials in the open, the danger
when all of it is stealing, taking,
when none of it by rights
comes to you, and you felt
for the maker, who had become absent,
when you saw the nest in the grass
coming apart in its hollow, its handful
of rest, where the not-work
could begin, where sleep
could start. The maker, there was
no sign of her, but in the nest, the three
children, those the nest

was made for, their eyes had never
opened, you thought of a potter
who stopped when the vessel had enough,
had become a series of circles
pressure allowed to become
grafted onto each other.
Even though clay is a different material.
Pine needles and bits of paper.
Recognized strands of your own hair.
Even though the mother is not
a human creature and so bears
no likeness to the artisan
we call a potter, her beak furrowed
into the soft body of her chick,
still making after the nest is done,
saying, in a language of pure pitch,
the next trick will be flight,
you have to do it yourself.

EULOGY

Morning, brilliant light, the arms of the lawn chair
and the exhaustion of the eyes, the edges
of the yard pintucked into place,
the root of the orange
tree, and the earth filled with sweet alyssum
hinges on it, like a human hip bending to pick a coin up.
My father is writing my mother's eulogy.

She isn't dead. Last night was the last
night of language, words had
already stopped, days before, but last night,
it appeared she discovered a new
language, in blinks she asked
for coffee, then, for the first song
from the Bill Evans trio's *Waltz for Deby*.

Or we asked her and she said yes,
and yes looked like
both eyes shut at once. Under the sun
umbrella, beneath the nest,
my father has just finished writing
his account of her life, eloquent but very simple,
factual and correct, it does not pander

with jokes, as its writer is already liked. Habitual,
it shies from anecdote. A perfect wife,

she contains sweetness
but not as in sugar in cube form, not formal, but sweet
as in honey dissolved in lemon
juice for a sick friend
with a sore throat. I am also in his speech.

I say something that resolves death.
The yard fills with sentences
now, the yard accepts another hour of closer
sunlight. In the speech, I say
all time is extra. I say *we are lucky*
under palm trees. The imagery
that dominates my father's complex

diction is that of light. His draft
full of tiny crossings out. The mother robin
polices the nest with her absence—
she hides it, she knows gratitude
for safety can't save her,
it would be gratitude to a predator
for not eating her, and that's only as good as silence.

RIOT

The nest became a way to sit
quietly under the nest. You felt a ruckus
anywhere a flower grew,
a riot, a gathering escalating past
the legal and the state.

In *Felix Holt* by George Eliot,
a magistrate pulls out the Riot Act
and reads it, as the crowd
of workers envelops
the voice of the law.

They are paid just well enough
not to be too hungry to riot.
Pitchforks and all sorts of implements
turned into weapons, a chase, and the landowner
gets put back into his house.

Rhododendrons by the swimming pool
in the kind of blush
women improve at, staring
into cameras. Tomato plants
overgrown their trellis, months before August.

Not to mention all the flowers sent.
Harder to get bad news in the morning,

with an entire day to talk to.
The nest is a blueprint of the first-
ever halo, before the angels

learned to work with light,
when there was only material, when they hadn't figured out
touching wasn't necessary for flight, and the shoulders
of the soldiers of light, God's army
bent under the weight of their crowns.

FROM THE NEST

1.

To speak through a shut
door, to interrupt
dreams and turn the sounds
the sick mouth makes
into prayer, to find
a voice that carries beyond
where I can see
is what I must do.
An ocean of stone
surrounds the plot of earth
I call home, rafters
without roots I take
to have been made
by human
hands, the shade made
by hands, a tent to prevent
the abundant light from
becoming too much.
What I am made of
whispers, frays, is shed,
returns to the ground again.
The remains
of what I had been
gathered from drift

through the yard
so gently I imagine
enough for many
of us. To appreciate
the sturdiness of one's own
constitution while
recognizing the
tenderness of the materials
one has depended
on: this is breath.
The hollow I administer
must be for lives.

2.

Mostly, I forget
who made me
but I remember being
made, just as I remember,
my hollow assembled, the
pressure of having
to hold. I have been
told I began as an idea.
The materials do not
agree: I am not woven
but lashed together,
not fine, not even,
and my fray, my lilting
to the left makes me best
for the place I was
placed. Added
to, I changed. Voices
beneath me do not
affect me, save a tiny
tremble at my underneath
from the change
in breath, but they
terrify the one who,
I think now, must
be my maker,
and I shake with her
out of proximity.

3.

I remember emptiness like
I remember a mouth
picking a piece of me
from a pile of identical
leaves around
the formidable base
of a trunk. I don't
try not to remember
but when the story
starts again, it comes
through rustle, through
a light resistance
that nevertheless grows
in volume, like a rock
down a hill of
rocks, like a creek
freezing in its hidden
parts, unfreezing
in the light as if
for show. I remember
emptiness from
the point of view
of the mouth,
and the mouth
remembers me
as usable.

4.

I distinguish the dying from
the living by their prone
position. They are always
in bedrooms, and often in
the afternoon, in the kitchen
with the news
folded over the forehead,
or near the screen with a green
game going. So, more
than one dying
lives, in any dwelling, under
any roof, but at times, one
body lies down
with a hard conviction
in the midst of others
who are kept from
that. The pitches of other
voices rise when one maker
tries to steal the nest
of another, and they
call this jealousy.

5.

What I see
from a height,
others live
within. Inside
the body I see
the child,
and others
see embers,
ash, the ending
of summer,
the suspension
that will
soon here
take hold.
*I was not
a living
thing*, I will
say to the
earth,
when it is
time.
I contained
life,
and it
flew.

6.

When I realized
I was finished,
suspension
was my first
sensation, the air
underneath
me a current
that took
but nevertheless
buoyed.
Oh body larger
than myself
when the distance
between my
underside and
the earth was
eliminated,
my purpose
also stopped,
and the weight
inside me
became gravity.
Why did you
go, air, I
was at work
in you, I
believed, as

any mother
believes
you would be
the only way
to enter.

7.

To say I have lived
as pressure means to neglect
the spaces in between
the rushes and lashes,
the needles and
locks of pines
and hairs, to fail
to consider the air
that gets in to even
the thinnest layers
of the tightest nest.
As I began in
feeling sometimes I
even seek those
airy pathways,
those places where
the weaving
works as structure,
not coverage,
which flood
with darkness
when the weight
of what they were
made to support
grows,
distributes itself
equally, becomes
less delicate,
and disappears.

8.

I began
as a scattering—
had twist
in me, loft,
then, a claiming
of space, and space's
chastened, fairest,
headstrong only
daughter: place-
ment. Then,
a spiral,
a base that
acted like
a whirlpool
composed
with the consent
of water,
so that what
moved the air
and carried me
at first had
no direction
except
toward itself,
toward a
meeting so
Möbius it
never began
or ended. I ended
as walls.

9.

Most is the breath
just before it's let
out, or at
the moment
it could be, when
the brain
apprehends the fact
that air
could be
released. Most
of us fall
to earth,
many
of the creatures
whose weight
we endure
die
before
we fall, though
in some
sense
this
could be a good
fate, not
to have to hunt,
not to kill,
to be
only killed
for, only

killed for
as care.
I like it here,
safe on earth,
pushed
out of a great
height, still
fit for use, and since
capable
of another
life, waiting
for it.

THE ACCOUNTS

I.

The nest was at rest for a time, not being
made. Before the eggs were laid, it softened.
The robin sleeping. Inside the house,
the sound of laundry
in the dryer, the sound of a zipper
tumbling inside
the apparatus, and shirts with buttons,
as well as napkins
and a tablecloth printed with blueberries
and stalks of lily of the valley, oval,
for the table with claw legs
and extra leaves for guests.

II.

In one account, the angels come, their hands
emerging from their wings like sentences
staying, as long as it takes,
for the windows to go from indigo
to black, as long
as it takes for a breath to land in the base
of the belly, in the cavity
wisdom tells us wisdom comes from
or first dwells in, before it navigates

the narrows of the throat, becomes mantra,
becomes guttural, becomes spit to aspirate
the language the mouth makes.
The native obligation of this account
to its subject is care. The form
of music the wind chime makes
registers the commitment
of a furious system, filled with
conviction, to the continued
transformation of what
is. Do not ask what has been
lost. Ask what changed. An instrument
of will, the guitar echoes this, a chord,
more reminder than absolute, the hand
arouses but does not create the scale.
In this way what rests gets taken up.

III.

In another, the mind makes a decision
to end its disorder. The mind wants first
to end the face. The subject
has had enough, one too many
figures walking through the orchard, the call
and response of conversation
become an imposition on some other world
unbroken by the idea of separate bodies,
an idea one has never been convinced of,
and so now it is a relief to believe
what one has suspected, that separation
a trick of perspective, though such a revelation

does not undo the fatigue of existing
in the continuing illusions of others. And yet, the obligation
to be kind, to show interest in strangers
when they visit with flowers, to family
whose hands are empty, and to doctors,
not to mention the pain.

IV.

In the last account, the explosions
are too small to be seen, and oxygen
takes both thirst and hunger away
as it ceases to find a home in the lungs,
and the patient, having ceased to feel, ceases
to breathe, as the heart shuts down
before the brain and shuts
the dreaming down, the settling on a nest
of images, not feeling any form of distress.
The pathways to distress are blocked,
but the senses doubled, the ears know
the house more than they ever did,
whose clothes occupy the dryer,
which voice accompanies water.

V.

Angels be patient with this subject.
I know what she would say to you
if she could speak,

                    if she could see
you just inside the window whose top right
pane frames what we call a family,
when the almost mother bird
finishes what she is thinking about,
barely but still hidden from sight.
If you stopped to look at the nest
you would see a sleep so purposeful
the ladder of adoration would reverse
and you would stay on earth.

THE BODY

Was the body taken up by the angels?
The minister wore a caftan, an African design, quite red
and misunderstood the location of the plot.
The uncle who had not been asked to speak
at the rosary finally got his turn.
Who came earlier to dig the hole?

How deep and how wide was the hole?
Pallbearers are the opposite of angels,
earthbound, having a last turn
at handholding, their hands turn red.
Their purpose to hold and not to speak,
they stand and wait next to the plot.

What distinguished this particular plot
from other plots? The branches above the hole
make a canopy of shade. Did anyone speak
tenderly about that? Did the angels
think the snippet of scripture that was read
made sense? Did the mourners return

home the long way? Whose turn
was it to do the dishes? Who untangled the plot
(and was it a good one) of the last book she read?
When they were gone, who filled in the hole
with dirt? Who addressed the angels?
It only became my turn to speak

when everyone else forgot how to speak
to each other. To get there, you must turn
left at a statue of Victorian angels.
You must cross more than one identical plot.
At the end of the day, you will see the whole
peninsula, from the rise of that hill, turn red.

Who will remember her birth, the streak of red
in her hair? I have wanted to speak,
I have wanted to tell the hole
to close, to become ground, to tell her to turn
into earth, to ease into the plot.
I have nothing to say to the angels.

Oh, the angels speak honey but their throats are red,
their plots are cunning, they are like us,
they talk and their faces turn into holes.

RADIATION

"His eye is on the sparrow."

They are letting you come back to me now.
I have to wait here, in front of the picture
on the screen of your brain
lit up like an entrance.

I prefer the word *sickness*
to the word *illness*.
A doctor treating a patient is like a person
who can't talk addressing an animal
who can't hear.

You are not looking for me. You are
getting your things together, the thinking
at the corners of your eyes, narrowing
on the buttons of your cardigan.

At the speed of someone blinking
on the first day warm enough
to wear a cotton sweater
the picture of your brain
changes to another picture
of your brain a fraction of a fraction
of a centimeter further from your forehead.

My hand holds a cup of coffee steady.
Is it what you want, the bitter
sun of it, the unset scandal of a sun
staying in the sky for one whole year,
not giving up its office,
abolishing elections, imprisoning the moon
and all the members of the moon's party?
I know what you hate: milk and sugar.

Do you know there is a table I lie on
every day to wait, trying to be patient,
for a machine that has to kill the good
alongside the bad, but should kill not enough good
to kill me for good, and cannot find
enough bad to make me whole
and unwrecked again?
I call it work and I call work
the meaning of the memory of disaster.

The technicians want to help you
but you walk out alone.
We leave the waiting room. We leave its puzzle
of the world, with all the husbands
working on it. Radiation is in the basement.
Someone has donated a garden. You will not take my arm.
Your eyes are on the flowers.

Three   I Am the Middle

I AM THE MIDDLE

I am looking at a picture
of my brother and my sister and myself
from before my brother
could read or write, the three of us
around a trash can, arms full of leaves

that have fallen on the front yard
because even in California, every property
has a bit of that season, one deciduous
tree. My sister on the right,
but in the corner of the picture, happy to do work,

her corn-colored hair whiter against the piles
of rust and blush and sunset, shining,
though effortless, she
organizes the picture, her pile
looks manageable, like she's holding

down the crackle. My brother, one hand
on the can, knows how to make
himself a part of the action, a token
leaf held in his right hand. He understands
he will be in a picture.

The leaves I hold are equal to myself
in amount, not weight. In volume

not shape. They are farthest from the can.
I look like I have eaten too much,
or like I don't know what work is.

Above me the cut half of an oak branch
shines its *O*, a shade darker than the side yard
where all the ivy started, the undergrowth
the lawn had to fight back.
I am the furthest back. I am the middle.

FROM THIS HOUSE THAT HOUSE

From this house that house
looks like a ship, through
these windows those shingles
are fins for a finer air, a fiercer
atmosphere. From California

Massachusetts looks like earth,
like it came first, in a time when
not every tree was asked to
make fruit. From a bent spine,
the practitioner comes up,

raises the world with her and at the end
of practice lies
down again. I knew time
because what I did
could improve, and persistence

of existence equals time,
as in served, or lived.
From a servant's
position, the life of the master
is cake, sweet,

from sweetness's position,
I mean, a pineapple

field, the car
we came in feels
so far away. From Christmas

to Easter abstemiousness
doesn't grace the year, we're
eating with the kings
that whole time, the Savior
is ours. From this bed,

the world equals the ship,
moving, and we equal
the ocean, and the window
is the moon telling
us to roll.

EARTH

When I was a little girl, all the time,
people asked me why I was sad.
I befriended a slug the same size
as my finger, but colder.
I followed the sound of my mother's keys.
When they went dark places, I hid.
My father bought baby roses
home for my mother: an anniversary.
I was sure they were for my teacher,
who held my hand when I wrote
the alphabet, but said *good work*
like what I did was mine.
In a warm climate, a longing for rain
came to me immediately.
Answering no question,
I was trying to be what they saw.

CONFESSION

A stripe of asphalt keeps the pond,
at the municipal park
in the capital of the state, in check. I went
there, going and coming
from your dying, to watch the ducks.

I mean I went there
to see a friend. On the way
to him I stopped at an orchard
and pistachios the color of oranges
are what I bought.

Kindness to those who keep
the sweetest secrets and long
life. Now that you
are dead, I can tell you
he was not a friend.

When we met, I could forget
you would not be.
Elsewhere, the orders
kept their orders through the fall.
I rose from the bed, the spring dismantled, he and I met

in secret and we spoke of how we wanted
to die like it was work.
Awake, I said, *yes*, driving him
on a road through green fields.
Painlessly, he said.

ARGUMENT ABOUT SILENCE

It was a hard house to live in for that season

You'll blame my pessimism, and then

because of the hole in the roof

you'll blame my temperament

caused by the pine tree cracking in half and falling

as if the two were different, as if I

on a morning in August when nothing else

could change who I wanted

happened, a day just like

to become, could change

the day from my childhood, before I could talk

the nose on my face

we found a two-headed snake

or my left-handedness

trying to eat itself

my teacher tried to change that

under the same tree

and failed.

ANIMALS

On Raymond Street, across from the park
where the Christmas lights stay up
all year, a girl says to her mother
that the piece of cake she ate with a scoop
of ice cream on top was as big
as the Great Wall of China.

How do you know about the Great Wall of China?
the mother asks, turning
her bicycle around, not a young mother
but healthy, she takes care
of herself, she has her own bike for training,
not just for riding with her daughter.

The girl does not think
this is a real question. You can tell by her face,
in the middle of what comes next so completely.
She says, with enthusiasm, *we pinned
the tail on the donkey.*
I understand the love for the donkey,

like you could love it without thinking
of being pinned, like the pinning the tail part
and the donkey part stayed separate.
Not even that reality and make-believe

stayed separate, but that pinning
wasn't the only way to touch the donkey.

When I was that girl's age, I played
an easier game. At school, on someone's birthday,
we got to write on the chalkboard.
The competition was to list
as many animals as we could name
inside a minute.

I knew *cat* and *dog*. Then I wrote *jackal*.
How did you know that,
my teacher said. She wasn't satisfied
with the *World Book*
being the answer. She wanted to know
who let me understand what I had found.

The mother and the daughter ride off together,
into the world behind the park, where the daughter
can't go alone, under the lights,
through a corridor of maples. They have trouble
hearing each other because of their helmets.
But they look forward, they've done this

before, I watch them
from the four-way stop where no one stops
completely but strangers.
The four-way stop, oracle of accidents,
something concrete to obey,
equal distributor of delay.

ARGUMENT ABOUT RESPONSIBILITY

The child doesn't remember all
the times you took her, she remembers

I spent a night in jail

the time you said you would
take her and you didn't

in the Central Valley of California,
at Christmastime,
for trying to drive across a bridge,

A pattern doesn't get formed

under the influence
that's what my sweat smelled like.
After they put the handcuffs on

by breaking but by all the times
before that though the breaking
makes us see

I saw the greedy winter fingers
of almond trees. When I looked back, the officers,
a woman and a man, had their hands
on my wrists where the cuffs would go.

The arrest wasn't fast. Like many
before me, I cried

responsibility

as they read me my rights, I misunderstood
them, talking the whole way

The year of your birth is not negotiable.

or knew them at once not to be
rights, but some form
of introduction

This is called chance,

an instruction manual
for those on law's other side.
A citizen is not the best of criminals.
My crime, as I said, was

we also call it accident,

recklessness

but I would like my crime to be ecstasy,
a more than healthy
appreciation of the manner
in which my lover bent my legs over
my shoulders in his pursuit
of proximity to my golden hair.

I'd like my conviction to reflect that.

Why should it matter to the law
which name to call me
if they have me bound?

a child never understands what a parent
goes through to make a pattern

since I didn't keep silent, it's the least they can do

until a child is a parent

until three springs come and the state erases me

it sounds like a form of punishment

(those almond trees, their bridal anxieties,
those blossoming months, sweet months before harvest)

but it's historical—

ARS POETICA: FUCHSIA

The music of free verse is easier
than the music of the sonnet. Which is why
I have avoided sonnets
in speaking of my mother—
to make the difficulty louder.

At the Citadel, the military
academy in South Carolina, one teacher
of composition forbid, for years,
the passive voice, calling it
womanly, across the fifties

and then, in the sixties, changed
the accusations he flung at grammatical
offenders to *homosexual*, though
for the most part, he used the derogatory
colloquial: *pansy*.

My mother was raised in the fifties
by a woman with impeccable manners
in a house full of crosses. On Sundays,
she covered her extremities
with white gloves and black mantillas.

In the picture I have of her
in her going-away

outfit, plaid, with a slender belt,
on her wedding day, her expression
marries confidence and disbelief,

looking at a friend, while my father
looks directly at the camera.
I want to look like that.
I loved the alphabet,
when I was a girl.

On the wall of my room,
fairies named after flowers
stood for every letter.
After much deliberation,
I decided to be Fuchsia.

GODS

Those whom the news has not yet reached
sit in the house
where you once soundly slept,

over greens and brown
rice, healthy in middle
age, considering

whether to put to sleep
the dog whose flatulence
shows her kidneys

to be kaput. Those
whom the news has not yet
reached do the dishes

themselves, the man
and the woman, dividing
the labor

equally, slowly, here
they bring the
mismatched dishes

up to the sink,
the counter of sparkling
granite, pink

from a cliff that faces the sea.
They have been talking about you,
and your age

is what they have been
talking about, your favorite
food, what to give

you for your
birthday, how to
celebrate the Fourth

of July with you,
when to see you next
if not the holiday.

His beard, his pointed
intellect, his compassion, the country
of his birth, his birth, her

bright, brown eyes
a shade less dark than
maple

bark, her desire
to ask questions, her need
to possess whatever happened

to you, her shape.
The news hasn't reached them yet.
And they sit,

by the pond that asks for
many adjectives, considering
your future,

with the leisure of gods.

WINTER

I wanted to write a poem
about something that hadn't happened
yet, like having
a child, or writing a sonnet
without rhymes hoping rhymes

might yeast on their own
and rise. But the poem—about taking
the canoe on Cook's Pond
in some future October
at twilight. Forever

off course, I find any drift more force-
ful than an argument,
or progress, I have a hunch a story's end
insults itself. The craft I meant
to handle, long and green,

with rust on the hull where one summer's
coat of paint peeled off leaving
another summer's leafier
green that other
hands had oared

faithful as safety and
visible

for all these months
out the back window
of this house where I am a winter

visitor, fortunate, to be present
in such warmth. In the faith that raised
me the son expires and the father never
has to, as the father never requires
getting saved. I thought

when I took the boat
the track I cut
could be a tether, a tail
without feathers, an arrow,
the width of an aspen though an aspen

would point upward, skyward
to the only place
where borders
can't be erased because
they disappear. A route, that track,

attaching me to shore, that on the clearest
day I could advance
from where I came from sure
that on the other side of all that was
visible I'd find nothing

different to approach but a world,
not even more lush, the same wind
through the same firs, where

another house left out
a red canoe. It was in winter

mother's telegraph lost
track of messages as the illness
came back. In the faith,
Mary wept like an expert, losing just
enough beauty, leading the history

which was her future to argue
that women excelled at pain.
In decent weather, to stay supine
in the frailest craft, still
possible. I would do that

letting the water
tantalize the boat with my intent
to stay still as the sun came
down to my level
and past. But now, as far as I can tell,

the space between the drifts
of snow only starts a path
across thick ice. As if the walker had no intention
to keep on. The faith I learned:
to wait for but never demand

an answer back. Sound
of shoes on ice, on the island
to the left a light snaps on

in a rickety clubhouse, where they watch
(so it is said) pornography, where they end

their boyish evenings with a snowball
fight. To say of fate, it is a lock
on a box, the length of a shadow
of any body the falling afternoon
ignites. To consider

before the trees even have a chance
to bloom early in a warm snap the nature
of mistake. To write down, to make
stick, what she
could no longer see—my

life. It was my intent
to double back in a line
like a loop of thread, white
against black water, and return
through the needle

of the night as I would at last
have something to come
back to, as on every side the houses turned
to rectangles of light, not to be
extinguished until sleep.

SNAKE

The thunderstorm came like a pot boiling over and the color
of water was made by that, all of a sudden, a pigment
more tropical than dense with the reflection of light.
Everywhere the scent of at least five different kinds of plants
lifted up. The desert can't talk back but I believe
it breathes instead, breathes vivid when the water
wants it the water can't wait and it breathes back.
I turned and went into the house.
Under the dining room table, a snake.
Green with a yellow stripe bisecting its back.
Motion ate each centimeter of floor
and air, scared, it makes sense to say, though there
exists or existed no safer time ever in which that shape
wouldn't want to move, dead August being the exception
to this when heat makes molasses of all of us.
Why did I want to chase it out? I did, I got a rake and kept
making it make that beautiful scared
shape upon the floor, so clean.
Like two ice cubes rubbing each other
and too cold to melt. Nothing organized that fear.
Seeing the edges it found its way out.